WORLD WATCH

UNICEF

Steven Maddocks

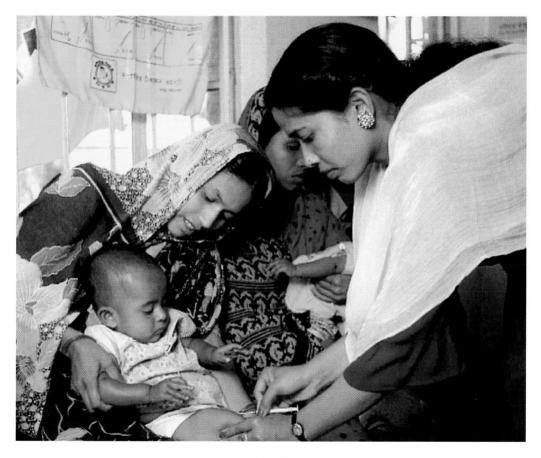

HODDER
Wayland

an imprint of Hodder Children's Books

WORLDWATCH SERIES

Greenpeace • Red Cross • UNICEF • United Nations • World Health Organization • WWF

Published for Hodder Wayland by White-Thomson Publishing Ltd,
2/3 St Andrew's Place, Lewes, East Sussex BN7 1UP

© 2003 White-Thomson Publishing

Published in Great Britain in 2003 by Hodder Wayland, an imprint of Hodder Children's Books.

Project editor: Nicola Edwards
Commissioning editor: Steve White-Thomson
Proofreader and indexer: Alison Cooper
Design: Jane Hawkins
Picture research: Tania Sentobe

British Library Cataloguing in Publication Data
Maddocks, Steven
   UNICEF. - (Worldwatch)
   1. UNICEF - Juvenile literature
   I. Title II. Edwards, Nicola
   362.7'0601
ISBN 0 7502 4336 8

Printed in Hong Kong
Hodder Children's Books, a division of Hodder Headline Ltd, 338 Euston Road, London NW1 3BH.

Picture acknowledgements: Cover UNICEF/HQ97-0302/Shehzad Noorani; title page UNICEF/HQ97-0302/Shehzad Noorani; p4© Abbie Trayler-Smith 2002; p7 UNICEF; p8 UNICEF/CP92/1/Roger Lemoyne; p9 UNICEF/S-012/33/David Barbour; p10 (SCF); p11 UNICEF/Ruby Mera; p12 UNICEF/Sonny Yabao; p14 UNICEF/92/Harriet Goodman; p16 UNICEF/HQ00-0076/Giacomo Pirozzi; UNICEF/HQ00-0205/Giacomo Pirozzi; p18UNICEF/C-115l/I dream of peace drawn by Adrijiana, Croatia; p19 UNICEF/96/Caroline Leveaux; p21 UNICEF UK/00Robert Aberman; p22 UNICEF UK/00Robert Aberman; p23 ©WTPix; p24 UNICEF/HQ95-0100/Ruth Massey; p26 UNICEF/HQ97-0302/Shehzad Noorani; p27 UNICEF/HQ91-0886/Lemoyne; p28 UNICEF/Horner; p29 UNICEF/91/Roger Lemoyne; p31 UNICEF/Carolyn Watson; p32 UNICEF Iraq; p34 UNICEF/92/J.Isaac; p35, p36 UNICEF Claudio Edinger; p37 UNICEF/5263/Jeremy Horner; p38 UNICEF/93-BOU0050Maggie Murray Lee; p40 UNICEF/ HQ99-0242/Jeremy Horner; p41 UNICEF/ HQ00-0786/Donna Decesare; p43 UNICEF/HQ96-0093/Giacomo Pirozzi; p44 UNICEF; p45 UNICEF/HQ02-0091/Donna Decesare.

Disclaimer: The website addresses (URLs) included in this book were valid at the time of going to press. However, because of the nature of the Internet, it is possible that some addresses may have changed, or sites may have changed or closed down since publication. While the author, packager and Publisher regret any inconvenience that this may cause readers, no responsibility for any such changes can be accepted by either the author, the packager or the Publisher.

This book has been checked by UNICEF for factual accuracy, but this is not a UNICEF publication and does not necessarily reflect the views or policy of UNICEF.

CONTENTS

Chapter One:
Immediate Response

• •

Late September 2001, at the UNICEF (United Nations Children's Fund) warehouse in Copenhagen, Denmark. Thousands of boxes of blankets, medical supplies and emergency food are loaded into cargo planes. Their destination: Afghanistan.

After three years of drought, and recent military action, the children of Afghanistan were facing a dangerous and freezing winter. The supplies had been bought with donations from people all over the world, after an appeal by UNICEF. Without them, thousands would die of illness and starvation.

It was impossible for the planes to fly above Afghanistan, so UNICEF gained permission to land in neighbouring countries. Somehow, the supplies would have to be transported into Afghanistan by land.

Over the Mountains

On 29 September, 200 tonnes of supplies arrived in Peshawar, Pakistan, 300 kilometres from the Afghan border. The supplies were loaded into 25 trucks, which headed north, towards the mountains. The roads were very basic, and with the added risk of heavy snow, the trucks were soon unable to continue. The supplies were moved onto 95 Jeeps. When even the Jeeps could go no further, the supplies were transferred again, onto hundreds of donkeys.

• •

On 21 March 2002, 1.5 million Afghan children officially went 'back to school'. In preparation for this day, UNICEF trained teachers, prepared facilities, and supplied equipment to nearly every school in the country. ▼

On 5 October, as winter began to set in, the goods finally reached their destination in Afghanistan. They helped to save the lives of thousands of children. But the need for UNICEF's help did not end there.

A Continuing Emergency

After decades of war, large numbers of children in Afghanistan live in areas where hospitals and schools have been bombed out of use. With no access to basic health care, many children fall sick and never recover. In the absence of schools – and girls were forbidden to go to school by the Taliban which ruled Afghanistan between 1996 and 2002 – there is little option but to find work, either in the home, on the land, or, most dangerous of all, as a soldier.

What Hope?

This book examines how UNICEF works to save and protect the world's children from the forces that threaten their lives, such as poverty, disease, war and lack of education. UNICEF needs time, the cooperation of politicians, the generosity of the world's more fortunate people, and most importantly, belief: the belief that if today's children are happy, healthy and safe, then tomorrow's world will be a better place.

ORGANIZATION IN FOCUS

Founded: 1946

Full name: The United Nations Children's Fund

Headquarters: New York

Executive Director: Carol Bellamy

Funding: Entirely by donations – 64% from governments, 36% from individuals and businesses

Employees: 5,554, from almost every nationality

Primary aim: UNICEF leads the worldwide campaign to respect children's rights, meet children's needs, and allow all the world's children, no matter what their race, gender or religion, to grow up in safety, freedom and good health.

Chapter Two:

Children First: A History of UNICEF

UNICEF was created in 1946, at the first meeting of the United Nations General Assembly. Since the nineteenth century, groups such as the International Red Cross/Red Crescent had been working to provide food and medicines for the victims of war, especially refugee families. However, UNICEF was the first Inter-Governmental Organization (IGO) to concern itself exclusively with children.

Innocent Victims

The notion that children need special protection has its origins in the first half of the twentieth century, when two devastating wars were fought in Europe. During the 1940s, former US president Herbert Hoover coordinated emergency food supplies in Europe.

Hoover visited thirty-eight countries, and found that war had left hundreds of thousands of families without homes and possessions. Twenty million children were undernourished, and killer diseases such as tuberculosis, rickets and anaemia were spreading rapidly. In the worst affected areas, half of all babies were dying before their first birthday. 'If Europe is to have a future,' Hoover declared, 'something must be done about those children.'

In 1943, the UK, USA, France and the Soviet Union, calling themselves the 'united nations', set up the Relief and Rehabilitation Administration (UNRRA) to help refugees.

FACTFILE: Children

- Every 15 minutes – the time it will take you to read this chapter – 311 children under 5 die in developing countries.
- Almost 11 million children under the age of 5 die each year.
- 26% of the population in developing countries live on less than $1 a day.
- At the dawn of the twenty-first century, the information age, 1 in 3 children in developing countries does not complete five years of basic education.
- 130 million children don't go to school.
- 211 million of the world's children (aged 5 to 14) work.

The Birth of UNICEF

In 1946, the UNRRA collapsed, mainly because the US had withdrawn its support. The United States had been providing over 70 per cent of the funding, but was unhappy that most of the aid was going to its new enemy, the Soviet Union.

Dr Ludwik Rajchman, a Polish delegate, was horrified. UNRRA had been providing essential relief for children across the world. The new, worldwide United Nations had just been created, and he campaigned for the establishment of an organization dedicated to bringing emergency relief to the world's sick and hungry children. As a result of Rajchman's efforts, all the UNRRA money was transferred to a new United Nations

▲ A poster for one of UNICEF's first campaigns, in 1946. Undernourished Austrian girls eat oranges, a vital source of nutrients. Early aid parcels also contained powdered milk, chocolate and biscuits.

International Children's Emergency Fund: UNICEF. Rajchman was appointed Chairman.

By 1950 UNICEF's attention had turned to child health in Asia, Africa and South America. During UN meetings in 1950, UNICEF's work was lavishly praised by the poorer countries who had benefited, and UNICEF was given three more years. Finally, in 1953, the UN created a permanent United Nations Children's Fund. The abbreviated name remained the same: UNICEF.

Early Success

In the 1950s, UNICEF noticed that, each year, millions of children were dying from illnesses which could be prevented with a single injection. UNICEF launched campaigns to immunize hundreds of millions of children against diseases like yaws and smallpox. These campaigns were great successes: smallpox no longer exists, and yaws is now very rare.

Development

In 1961 the US president, John F. Kennedy, told the United Nations General Assembly that it was the duty of the richer nations of the world to help 'those peoples in the huts and villages of half the globe struggling to break the bonds of mass misery'. The UN proclaimed the 1960s as 'The International Development Decade'. The year 1965 was a high point in UNICEF's history. The organization received the Nobel Peace Prize 'for the promotion of brotherhood among nations'.

Serving the Community

During the 1960s, it became clear to UNICEF that campaigns against specific diseases were only short-term solutions. To make a lasting impact on the basic health of children in poorer countries, it would have to address the root cause: poverty. In the years that followed, UNICEF broadened its work considerably. Its programmes ranged from well-digging to teacher-training. Development had to be sustainable, which means ensuring that after experts leave an area, the problem doesn't return.

A classroom in Cambodia. In 1979, UNICEF was one of the first international agencies to return to Cambodia, after the fall of the Khmer Rouge government, whose policies had led to the deaths of over two million people. ▼

◀ In 1990 UNICEF Executive Director James P. Grant organized the World Summit for Children, one of UNICEF's most impressive achievements.

leadership of James Grant, UNICEF made immense progress in child health.

Grant was the Executive Director of UNICEF from 1980 to 1995. He won the support of many of the world's most powerful leaders for his 'Child Survival and Development Revolution'. He believed that protecting children is basic and affordable, and that it helps a country to progress and develop.

For UNICEF's campaigns to succeed, it was important to get to the heart of the problem. UNICEF kept as many workers as it could in the target countries themselves, often in remote rural communities.

UNICEF stressed the importance of 'community participation'. The theory behind this is that the people who are in the best position to find and maintain a solution are those who are actually suffering.

The 1980s

During the 1980s disastrous harvests, civil wars, growing debts and the beginnings of HIV/AIDS deepened the suffering of many of the world's poor. The global population soared and the gap between richer and poorer nations widened. Yet, under the

In 1999, at Brussels National Airport in Belgium, two teenagers from Guinea-Conakry in West Africa were found dead in the landing gear of a plane. They had stowed away, hoping to escape to a new life. This is from the letter that was found on their bodies:

"Sirs/Madams, citizens and officials of Europe we are appealing to your solidarity and kindness to come to our rescue. Please, help us. We are enormously suffering in Africa. Help us, we have problems and those problems include the abuse of the children's rights.**"**

CHILDREN'S RIGHTS

The campaign for children's rights began with Eglantyne Jebb, who founded the Save the Children Fund in 1919. In 1923 this passionate and determined British woman drafted the 'Declaration of the Rights of the Child'. When it was adopted by the League of Nations (the predecessor of the UN) as the 'Declaration of Geneva', it was the first document in history endorsed by the international community to state that children have rights.

At first UNICEF hesitated to join the campaign to fix the rights of children firmly in international law. The organization was concerned that it would need to devote a large proportion of its time and money to complex legal negotiations. UNICEF is valued for its political neutrality, and this might also have been compromised.

However, under James Grant, UNICEF joined the campaign for a legally-binding international children's rights treaty. The UN proclaimed 1979 the 'International Year of the Child'. The Government of Poland made an official proposal to the United Nations

After the First World War, Eglantyne Jebb was accused of helping the enemy. She replied, 'My Lord, I have no enemies below the age of 11.'

"If children are allowed to grow up … ignored in their misery by the more fortunate, they will inevitably grow up to hate and destroy, and tomorrow's world can only end up in disaster."

Eglantyne Jebb, Declaration of the Rights of the Child, 1924 – the world's first children's rights document.

Commission on Human Rights, which began drafting a treaty. Ten years of painstaking work by the member states of the UN followed.

The Convention on the Rights of the Child

On 20 November 1989, the UN officially adopted the United Nations Convention on the Rights of the Child. The Convention was opened for signature on 26 January 1990, and a record 61 countries signed it on that day.

By 2002, 191 out of 193 countries had ratified the Convention. This means they have formally agreed to observe it. If the two remaining

countries, the US and Somalia, were to ratify, the Convention on the Rights of the Child would become the first universal law of mankind.

Key Principles

The Convention serves to protect every child in the world, no matter what his or her race, religion, language or culture.

The 54 articles of the Convention cover many categories. Children have survival rights – including the right to food, shelter and health care; development rights – including the right to education, safe play and freedom of thought; rights to protection from all forms of abuse and rights to participation in decisions which affect their lives.

Crucially, the Convention also says that children have the responsibility to respect the rights of others.

Former Russian president Boris Yeltsin signs the World Summit for Children Declaration and Plan of Action in 1990. ▼

Chapter Three:
How UNICEF Works

It is a sad fact that each year in the developing world, hundreds of thousands of babies die in their first six months of life from disease and malnutrition.

BABY-FRIENDLY HOSPITALS

After much work in this area UNICEF and the WHO (World Health Organization) launched the Baby-Friendly Hospitals Initiative in 1992. To become officially 'Baby-Friendly', maternity hospitals all over the world had to fulfil ten criteria. One of the most important was to pass on information about correct

A mother and child taking part in a Baby Friendly initiative in the Philippines. ▼

breastfeeding. The staff were also required to provide appropriate care and support for mothers.

Within ten years, more than 14,500 hospitals in 128 countries had been transformed, with over a million people working under the scheme. Worldwide there were dramatic reductions in illness and mortality in infants. For example, in Chile in 1985, only 4 per cent of babies were fed on breast milk alone in the first six months of life. In 1996 the figure was 40 per cent.

GRASS ROOTS

Although the Baby-Friendly Hospital Initiative was a worldwide campaign, UNICEF implemented it differently in each country, according to the country's needs.

UNICEF country offices run their campaigns independently. They recruit volunteers, and team up with local non-governmental organizations (NGOs) and charities, who have special knowledge of local culture. The emphasis is on training, ensuring that correct information is passed down through the generations, so that change becomes permanent.

A criticism of many global organizations is that too much of their money is swallowed up simply in running the organization itself. UNICEF's success is based on its unique 'field-based' structure. This means that 85 per cent of UNICEF staff are 'out in the field' in the countries which need them, rather than in offices.

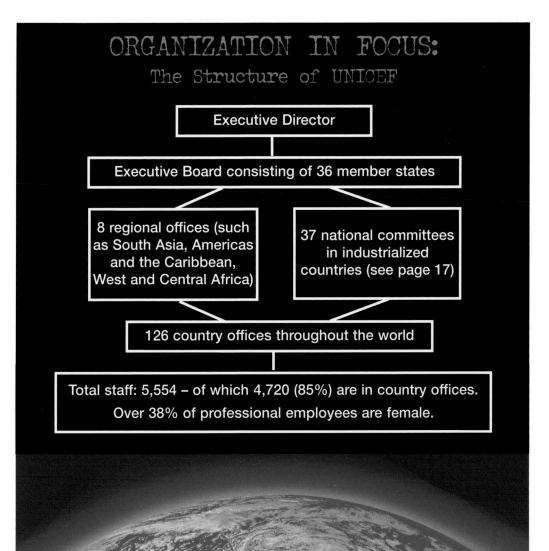

ORGANIZATION IN FOCUS:
The Structure of UNICEF

Executive Director

Executive Board consisting of 36 member states

8 regional offices (such as South Asia, Americas and the Caribbean, West and Central Africa)

37 national committees in industrialized countries (see page 17)

126 country offices throughout the world

Total staff: 5,554 – of which 4,720 (85%) are in country offices. Over 38% of professional employees are female.

CHANGING THE RULES

Many African and Asian countries simply do not have the money and resources to create good health and welfare systems for all people. As a result, the poorest people, and those who live far from the big cities, have no access to primary health care – basic medicines and advice.

UNICEF aims to make a lasting difference to the health of children in developing countries. To achieve this, laws need to be changed, and health services need to be reformed. One of UNICEF's tasks is to persuade governments to commit themselves to such changes.

THE BAMAKO INITIATIVE

Launched in 1987, the Bamako Initiative was a campaign which asked African governments to rethink their national health programmes. UNICEF aimed to ensure that all African children had access to primary health care. The key was to persuade African governments to allow communities to run their own health services.

Helping People Help Themselves

The Bamako Initiative helped villagers set up rural health centres. UNICEF provided a basic stock of medicine and supplies and trained local health workers to give health advice for babies and children.

UNICEF's most valuable work takes place at the heart of the community. Here, a community nurse gives health advice to villagers in Kiberia, Kenya. ▼

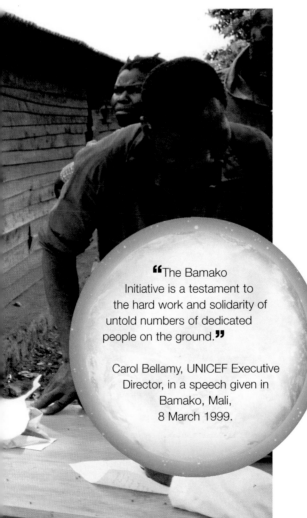

"The Bamako Initiative is a testament to the hard work and solidarity of untold numbers of dedicated people on the ground."

Carol Bellamy, UNICEF Executive Director, in a speech given in Bamako, Mali, 8 March 1999.

The medicine was not free, but it was affordable for local people. Many people in the affected communities had been paying for their health care anyway – and often receiving poor quality medicines or bad advice. Opponents argued that all children had a right to free health care, but this is simply not possible for many poor countries. A 1994 report confirmed that people would be willing to continue paying a reasonable fee for facilities – as long as the money stayed in the community.

Mixed Results

UNICEF country offices throughout Africa helped set up local health committees, elected by the villagers. The committees set local fees for the medicines and services, and made sure all the money was used to keep funding the health centres.

In the West African countries of Benin and Guinea, as a direct result of the Bamako Initiative, the percentage of children immunized against the six most lethal diseases went up from under 15 per cent in 1985 to 73 per cent in 1993.

However, in some countries, such as Swaziland in southern Africa, the charges put people off. UNICEF concluded that in some countries, the programme had not been planned or publicized well enough. UNICEF tries to learn from the successes and failures of all its initiatives.

PAYING FOR UNICEF

UNICEF is the only UN agency to rely entirely on donations. In the year 2001, UNICEF's total income was US$ 1.218 billion, with 64 per cent coming from governments. In 2001, the largest government donor was the US, which provided a total of US$ 216 million. In second place was Japan with US$ 98 million, and third was the United Kingdom with US$ 74 million.

The UN argues that a mere 0.7 per cent of the entire budget of industrialized countries should be given over to aid for developing countries. Currently, only four countries meet this level: Sweden, Norway, Denmark and the Netherlands. The average country gives only 0.39 per cent.

Around 33 per cent of UNICEF's income comes from non-government and private sources – companies, organizations and individuals. Major private donors include the Bill and Melinda Gates Foundation and Ted Turner's United Nations Foundation. Throughout the world, private funds are contributed mainly through UNICEF's national committees.

◀ Success: massive commitment of resources to emergency relief meant very few children died in the floods in Mozambique in March 2000. ▼

FACTFILE: Comparing Costs

UNICEF's total income 2001:	US$ 1.218 billion
Total cost of providing clean water and sanitation for everyone in the world:	$600 billion
Amount needed to provide all basic social services in developing countries:	$40 billion a year
Cost of a weight-for-height chart to help health workers detect malnutrition in children:	$25
Cost of buying enough vitamin A capsules to prevent 30 children going blind:	$1
Amount the world spends on playing golf:	$45 billion a year
Amount the world spends on cigarettes:	$100 billion a year

A Unique Network

Unlike any other UN organization, UNICEF has national committees. Working in industrialized countries from Andorra to New Zealand, these 37 committees often persuade national governments to change their policies and commit more money to helping children at home and abroad.

The national committees also raise funds and make it possible for everyone to contribute to improving the lives of children. Many of them – in Japan, Germany, and Greece, for example – raise more money than the amounts their governments provide.

Where the Money Goes

UNICEF's expenditures are recommended by the Executive Board, and authorized by the Executive Director. In 2001, total expenditure was US$ 1.246 billion. About 93 per cent of this sum was spent by country offices.

Keep Giving

One of UNICEF's greatest worries is donor fatigue. Every single year, individuals, companies and governments need to be persuaded once again to allocate a part of their budget to UNICEF. This takes continuing pressure, persuasion and publicity. Donors want to feel that their money is making a difference and being spent properly. Keeping its donors in mind, UNICEF continually aims to monitor and improve its effectiveness.

Chapter Four:
UNICEF's Challenges

Since its very earliest days, UNICEF has been forced to deal with the appalling consequences of war. At the beginning of the twenty-first century, the need is even greater. On any day, more than twenty armed conflicts are being fought around the world. Most of these conflicts are being fought in desperately poor countries. Tragically, on average, developing countries spend as much on their militaries as they do on health and education combined. All too often, the worst affected by this are children.

'Ghosts and skeletons in my closet' by Adrijiana, a 12-year-old girl from war-torn Croatia. At a UNICEF 'Education for Peace' class, Adrijiana was encouraged to express her feelings through art. ▼

THE HORRORS OF WAR

Since 1990, over two million children have been killed in conflict and six million have been left injured or disabled, especially by landmines.

Children who survive war may be left completely alone, their families killed and their schools bombed. Also since 1990, 12 million children have been made homeless by war. Young survivors frequently end up fending for themselves in the squalor and sickness of refugee camps, deeply traumatized by the terrible violence they have witnessed.

In refugee camps throughout the world from the Congo to Kosovo, UNICEF has created 'child-friendly spaces' where children can play, learn and try to come to terms with their experiences.

Days of Tranquillity

Health systems often collapse in war zones, especially if they were only in the early stages of development anyway. Immunizing children in war zones is one of the toughest challenges UNICEF faces.

UNICEF campaigns for 'Days of Tranquillity'. On these days, fighting must stop, and planners and health workers must be given the free run of the country. Incredibly, during the 1990s, UNICEF managed to negotiate 'Days of Tranquillity' in some of the world's most war-torn countries, such as the Sudan, El Salvador, Afghanistan and Sri Lanka.

Child Soldiers

In many war zones, children are not simply witnesses to horrific violence. They may be made to participate as child soldiers. Some child soldiers are as young as 8. Many are killed. Most who survive never recover from the terrible experience.

▲ Children injured by landmines. Costing as little as $2, some landmines are only the size of an orange, but can easily blow off a leg. They kill or maim 8,000 to 10,000 children each year.

An Olive Branch

UNICEF does all it can to persuade warring parties not to recruit soldiers under the age of 18. In many cases, these are armed rebel groups who obey no internationally recognized 'rules of war'. Yet UNICEF has to convince them that the welfare of children is important enough for them to change their practices.

In 1995, the Sudan People's Liberation Movement, the main, rebel group in southern Sudan, signed 'Ground Rules'. This was a document, drawn up by UNICEF and local NGOs, which included a commitment to the UN Convention on the Rights of the Child.

MOTHER LOVE

UNICEF has always recognized that the mother is by far the most important factor in a baby's survival, providing essential health, nutrition and care. Yet, in many societies throughout the world, discrimination against women makes it difficult for them to be good mothers.

Discrimination begins early in life. Girls, more often than boys, are underfed, overworked, and denied access to school. Of the 120 million children in the world without access to basic education, the majority are girls.

Without proper education, girls are less able to stand up for their rights, and more likely to experience poverty and exploitation. At the same time, young boys are brought up to consider girls inferior to them (see page 33).

Too Much Too Young

In some cultures, families believe women are made only for marriage and motherhood. In some Asian countries, 50 per cent of girls are married off by their fifteenth birthday and 65 per cent of women have a baby before they are 20 years old.

In some traditional societies, girls have little choice over the use of their bodies. Many teenage pregnancies are the result of rape. The risks of teenage pregnancy are very high – in many cases, the girl's body is not yet ready to give birth. Worldwide, pregnancy complications are the main cause of death for 15- to 19-year-old girls. In addition, many developing countries do not provide women with safe, hygienic birth conditions.

UNICEF estimates that as many as 4.4 million teenage girls have abortions every year. Most of them

FACTFILE: Reproductive Health

- Every year, 585,000 women die during pregnancy or childbirth; of these, 99% are in developing countries.
- Each year, there are 3 million stillbirths. Another 3 million babies die in their first week.
- In some parts of the developing world, teenage pregnancies account for up to 20% of births.
- A baby born to a mother younger than 17 has a 60% greater chance of dying before its first birthday than a baby born to a mother older than 20.

are in developing countries, in unsafe conditions. In several countries, like Nigeria, teenagers who undergo illegal abortions account for half of all maternal deaths – women who die during pregnancy, childbirth, or shortly afterwards.

▲ Carol Bellamy, Executive Director of UNICEF. INSET: The UNICEF logo, a mother and a baby silhouetted against a background symbolizing world peace. UNICEF sees the health, nutritional wellbeing, education and rights of a woman as crucial to the survival of her children.

Supporting Women

In all of its programmes, UNICEF emphasizes the equal rights of males and females. UNICEF legal teams help countries introduce legislation to ensure that girls are as well provided for as boys.

UNICEF aims to give young women alternatives to having babies, by encouraging them to stay in school as long as possible and maximize their career opportunities. UNICEF-supported education programmes in schools and family-planning clinics teach girls about reproductive health. Maternity clinics are properly equipped, and health workers are properly trained. Finally, UNICEF seeks to overturn discrimination against women by placing women at the centre of all of their initiatives, from setting up health centres to installing water pumps. In 1995, UNICEF insisted that its new Executive Director – only the fourth in fifty years – be a woman.

21

◀ In many countries, people are afraid to talk about AIDS. UNICEF works to encourage everyone to discuss AIDS openly and honestly. Here, British pop star Robbie Williams, a UNICEF UK Special Representative, promotes the importance of 'breaking the silence'.

HIV AND AIDS

AIDS is a disease which attacks the immune system and always leads to death. HIV is the infection which eventually develops into AIDS. HIV is transmitted when two people have very intimate contact with each other, if they exchange blood (for example, by sharing needles) or other bodily fluids (for example, during sexual intercourse).

AIDS represents the biggest disaster humanity has ever faced. There is no cure for AIDS, so the most important defence UNICEF can mount is to stop people getting it in the first place.

Breaking the Silence

AIDS overwhelmingly affects the young. Half of the world's infections occur in people aged under 25. Tragically, hundreds of thousands of young people are infected simply because they have not been told about the risks of HIV.

UNICEF's field-based structure enables it to work, through its country offices, at the heart of communities. In Lao PDR in South East Asia, for example, monks are influential and respected figures in the community. With the support of the Association of Buddhist Clergy, UNICEF ran the Mettha Dhamma ('compassionate teaching') project, to train monks to offer HIV/AIDS education.

Helpless Victims

HIV can be transmitted from a pregnant mother who is infected to her baby in the womb. HIV-infected babies rarely survive into childhood. Every day, 1,600 babies and children die of AIDS.

Many mothers, whose bodies have been weakened by HIV, do not survive long after giving birth. Their babies are left infected and alone.

Growing Up Alone

The majority of people who die of AIDS are parents of young children. In Uganda, 1 in 15 children under the age of 15 has been orphaned by AIDS. Across Africa, the heart has been ripped out of families, leaving elderly

FACTFILE: HIV and AIDS

- In Africa, 25% of women attending antenatal clinics are HIV-positive.
- One in three babies born with HIV does not survive beyond its first birthday.
- In sub-Saharan Africa, 11 million children have seen one or both of their parents die from AIDS.
- Worldwide, 14 million children – more than all the children in the UK – have been orphaned by AIDS.
- Almost 25 million people have been killed by AIDS; nearly five million of them were children under 15.
- Every minute, four young people become infected with HIV.
- It is estimated that 1 in 9 people in Zambia is HIV-positive.
- Kofi Annan, the UN Secretary General, in May 2001 called for a five-fold increase in spending on the war against AIDS.

grandparents or young children in charge of households, with little hope of bringing in any money.

UNICEF does all it can to support orphans and affected families. Through community programmes, such as Uganda's AIDS Widows, Orphans Family Support organization (AWOFS), working in conjunction with the Ugandan Catholic Church,

UNICEF helps families stay together and generate income. With the support of programmes like AWOFS, children can continue to go to school. Despite their tragic experiences, such children may have a better chance in life.

▼ A march in Kenya to raise awareness of HIV/AIDS. In 2002 there were 1.1 million AIDS orphans in Kenya.

Chapter Five:
UNICEF Campaigns

In the early 1980s, in villages across the east African country of Tanzania, babies and young children in their thousands were falling ill and dying. Those who survived grew up weakened for life. Their mothers had no idea why.

Health experts decided that the problem was malnutrition. As a result of their poor diet, the children's bodies were not strong enough to fight off simple illnesses. Infant deaths were especially high in the Iringa region of central Tanzania. Yet in Iringa, there was a good supply of basic food. UNICEF realized that the children were not starving to death – they were just not being fed properly.

THE HIDDEN HUNGER

In 1984, together with the World Health Organization (WHO), UNICEF launched the Child Survival and Development Programme in Iringa. They campaigned for funding, and the Italian government made a huge donation. The UNICEF country office in Tanzania sent teams of workers out into the affected communities. They took with them a specially-made educational video, called *The Hidden Hunger*.

The Heart of the Problem

Malnutrition is not something you can 'see'. However, malnourished babies do not grow as quickly as healthy babies. If only the mothers could be taught to monitor their children's growth, perhaps they could help their babies to stay healthy.

'Weighing posts' were set up in the villages. Every three months there was a Health Day, run by Tanzanian health workers. The mothers of the village brought their children to be weighed and measured. The child's growth was recorded on a chart, and mothers compared their charts.

◀ A weighing post in the Sudan. UNICEF applied the principles of its Iringa programme to countries throughout Africa.

St. BENEDICT SCHOOL
DERBY
DE22 1JD

In Control of Their Own Lives

UNICEF wanted to make sure that when the aid workers moved on, the problem didn't return. Training and education were essential. Parents and health workers were taught how to check on the health of the children and to take any necessary action.

The Child Survival and Development Programme did not change anything about the basic food supply in Iringa. Ways of combating malnutrition included feeding children more often, learning how to make a nutritious porridge and making the home more hygienic.

The programme was expanded until it covered more than half of Tanzania. In the affected villages, severe malnutrition was virtually eliminated, and there was a huge reduction in mild and moderate malnutrition. Throughout the 1980s and 1990s, UNICEF set up similar programmes throughout the world.

FACTFILE: Malnutrition

- Around 150 million children in developing countries are malnourished.
- In developing countries, 11 million children under the age of 5 die every year. Malnutrition contributes to over half of those deaths.
- Stunted growth affects 226 million children worldwide.
- Worldwide, 67 million children are wasted (underweight).
- In South Asia, 50% of children are underweight.
- In the US, 20% of children live in poverty.
- One in every four American children under 12 has problems getting the food he or she needs.
- In Central Asia, 60% of pregnant women and young children are anaemic.

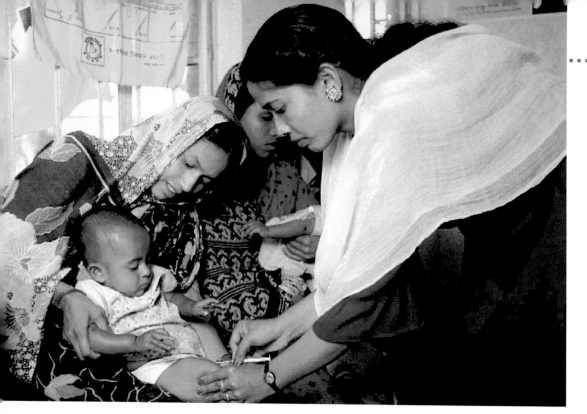

HEALTH FOR ALL

At UNICEF's 40th Anniversary Conference in 1985, Executive Director James Grant reaffirmed UNICEF's commitment to 'Universal Child Immunization'. Sustained efforts by UNICEF, the WHO, Rotary International and more than 10 million volunteers in 100 countries led to what has been described as 'the greatest global mobilization in peacetime history'.

Vaccines

During the first year of life, babies need to be regularly injected with vaccines. The vaccines are medicines which give protection (immunization) against a range of infectious diseases, such as measles and polio. In the developing world, many governments do not have the resources to run vaccination programmes. As a result,

▲ A baby being immunized against tetanus at a community health centre in Bangladesh. UNICEF and the WHO have committed themselves to eliminating maternal and neonatal tetanus by 2005.

three million babies die each year from vaccine-preventable diseases.

Turkey's Example

In February 1985, James Grant obtained a commitment from the Turkish Prime Minister, Turgul Ozal, to reduce the number of unvaccinated children in Turkey. The campaign leaders announced that 45,000 vaccination posts would be required, and 12,000 health staff and 65,000 volunteers would have to be trained.

The mothers of five million children would have to be persuaded to bring their babies to be vaccinated not

once, but three times. Vaccines would have to be delivered to remote, mountainous regions with no roads and – making things even more difficult – with no electricity. Vaccines need to be kept refrigerated until use in order to be effective.

A Country Mobilized

By July, the President of Turkey had secured the commitment of all 67 provincial governors, and also 200,000 teachers, 54,000 imams (Muslim mosque leaders) and 40,000 muhtars (village leaders). The meat and fishing industries had offered their refrigeration facilities. Constant radio and television announcements reached 30 million homes.

At the televised launch, the President, the Prime Minister, the Chief Imam and James Grant each vaccinated a baby. Throughout the campaign, nightly reports on TV and

▲ Temperature-controlled vaccines at UNICEF's warehouse in Copenhagen. UNICEF spends over US$ 100 million a year on vaccines and needles, making it the world's largest purchaser.

radio gave progress updates. Vaccines were transported around the country, sometimes carried on horseback after being stored in shop fridges.

By November, 84 per cent of the target group had been immunized, hailed by UNICEF as proof that it is possible to engage a whole society when children are the cause.

FACTFILE: Immunization

1990 World Summit For Children, Goal 22:

At least 90% of children under one year of age to be immunized against diphtheria, pertussis, tetanus, measles, poliomyelitis and tuberculosis by 2000.

Percentage of children worldwide immunized in

1974:	5
1990:	73
1999:	72

> **"** Potentially the most important medical advance of the century. **"**
>
> Description of ORT by the British medical magazine, *Lancet*.

ORAL REHYDRATION THERAPY

During the early 1980s James Grant identified four priorities in the area of primary health care. He called his priorities GOBI. G stood for Growth Monitoring, B was for Breastfeeding and I was for Immunization. The O stood for Oral Rehydration Therapy (ORT), a treatment for diarrhoea.

Diarrhoea is caused by any upset to the digestive system, especially brought on by drinking dirty water. The body tries to flush out any poisons. During the process, a lot of the body's water is used up. Dehydration causes 90 per cent of diarrhoea-related deaths.

Oral Rehydration Salt (ORS) is a simple combination of glucose and salt. Mixed with clean water it replaces everything the body loses during bouts of diarrhoea. Grant carried a packet of ORS in his pocket wherever he went, promoting the cause of ORT tirelessly until his death in 1995.

The Worst Enemy

Health experts learned that, due to lack of information, many mothers throughout the developing world were stopping all feeding of their babies during bouts of diarrhoea.

◀ A health worker in Peru treats a baby suffering from diarrhoeal dehydration. The packets in the foreground contain ORS.

This is the worst possible course of action because the body's water and nutrients must be replaced.

Diarrhoea kills a child every 15 seconds. Around 1.5 million children under the age of 5 in developing countries die every year from diarrhoea. ORT could prevent 90 per cent of these deaths. It isn't really diarrhoea that kills these children: it is one of UNICEF's worst enemies – lack of knowledge of the proper treatment.

Get the Message?

Public education was once more a key to UNICEF's campaign to widen usage of ORT. UNICEF's goal was to ensure that family doctors and health workers prescribed ORT in all cases of diarrhoea, and gave appropriate advice to mothers. Radio and television campaigns encouraged people to put pressure on their doctors. In India, the UNICEF television campaign explained that ORT was cheap, simple and effective. It said that 'modern' doctors use it, and 'If your doctor is modern, then he should be using it too'.

In Mexico, a television commercial explained that the vast majority of children who died from diarrhoeal dehydration had visited a private doctor shortly before their death. Whatever advice and remedy the doctors were providing, it was not helping. Doctors in Mexico responded immediately. In 1995, Mexico had an 80 per cent usage rate of ORT.

A billboard in Cameroon, advertising ORT. The UNICEF goal for ORT use in 80 per cent of diarrhoea cases was achieved by about 25 developing countries by the end of 1995. ▼

WATER AND SANITATION

More than a billion people lack access to clean drinking water and roughly 2.5 billion people do not have access to sanitary toilet facilities. As a result, families have to drink dirty water, and are unable to follow basic hygienic practices, such as washing their hands and disposing of their waste properly.

Among the most serious consequences is disease, particularly dysentery and cholera, which are often fatal. Children are the most vulnerable: there is a direct link between poor sanitation and child mortality.

UNICEF's Response

Article 24 of the Convention on the Rights of the Child obliges countries to recognize a child's right to 'enjoyment of the highest attainable standard of health', and to provide 'clean drinking water … and environmental sanitation'. Many of UNICEF's campaigns have focused on this basic children's right. 'Sanitation for All by the Year 2000' was a key goal of the 1990 World Summit for Children.

In many parts of the world, however, it remains a long way off. Half of all people in Asia still have no access to basic sanitation. More and more people in the developing world are moving to overcrowded and dirty cities where the existing water and sanitation systems are unable to cope.

FACTFILE: Threats to Health

- Problems with water and sanitation lead to 21 out of the 37 major diseases affecting developing countries.

- In developing countries, three million child deaths a year – 1 in 4 – are related to water and sanitation.

- Worldwide in the year 2002, over 1 billion people had no access to safe water and nearly 2 billion people lacked safe sanitation.

- During the 1980s, $1 billion was invested annually on water and sanitation. However, 70% of the money was spent on high-cost projects for wealthier city-dwellers.

- Between 1990 and 2000, 816 million people gained access to safe water, and 747 million to sanitation.

- More children have been killed by diarrhoeal dehydration in the last ten years than all the children killed in armed conflict since the end of the Second World War.

The Problem of Planning

In remote rural areas, particularly in parts of Africa, India and China, a bucket of clean water may be several hours' walk away. It is usually girls and women who have to make the journey. Since the 1970s, UNICEF has supported a great number of well-digging programmes. However, not all of them have been successful.

Earlier wells tended to be technologically very complicated. They looked good, but when they broke down, no one knew how to fix them and no spare parts were available.

UNICEF and its partners realized yet again that programmes planned and set up by central authorities and then presented to the local people often fail. Such a way of working depends on stable governments and economies, which many developing countries do not have.

▲ UNICEF has helped communities to build their own low-cost hand pumps, like this one in Nepal, to draw water from the ground. The programmes have provided training in maintenance and repair.

Self Help

Community participation, on the other hand, means that local people can use local materials to create a system which suits them. This leads to a sense of ownership and pride, and a greater desire to help to make the programme succeed.

In countries as far apart as Myanmar, Guatemala and Sudan, UNICEF has supported sanitation programmes tailored to each community. In Myanmar, a UNICEF-assisted programme offered people a choice of latrines. Enthusiasm was so high that in one year, 800,000 families built their own latrines.

THE IMPORTANCE OF EDUCATION

In the developing world, cycles repeat themselves from generation to generation. For example, impoverished children are likely to become impoverished parents; malnourished girls are likely to become malnourished women and in turn give birth to underweight babies. UNICEF and its partners in development have long believed that education is the only way to escape these traps.

The Information Age?

The Gulf War in 1991 devastated Iraq, leaving large areas of the country without water, food or medicine. Since then, Iraqis have seen their country slide further into poverty and deprivation. The education system has suffered particularly. School buildings have collapsed and there are few properly-trained teachers.

▲ Iraqi children learn lessons for life. The right to a free primary education is set out in the UN Convention on the Rights of the Child. Educated girls improve not only their own life potential, but also that of their future families and of society as a whole.

In 2002 one in four of all school-aged children (6-15 years of age) were not attending school. Poverty is the main cause, and the main result: 23 per cent of Iraqi children aged between 6 and 15 have to work on the streets to supplement the money earned by other members of the family.

The situation in Iraq is becoming desperate. If today's children are not educated, there is a real danger that future generations of illiterate children will grow up in terrible circumstances. The threat of violence, hunger and disease will continue unchecked.

UNICEF's Action Plan

In conjunction with the Iraqi Ministry of Education and UNESCO (the United Nations Educational, Scientific and Cultural Organization), UNICEF's country office in Iraq is working to improve access to free primary education for all children.

During the year 2000, 728 schools were renovated or rebuilt. Around 690,000 children received stationery and 60,000 received desks. A total of 300 special two-classroom rural schools were built in remote villages.

Training

During 2000, UNICEF trained 2,600 teachers in Iraq. Teachers are trained to teach not only maths and languages (Arabic, Kurdish and English), but also health, hygiene, care for the environment and children's rights.

A further 3,000 teachers were trained to give some lessons on a vital subject in Iraq: landmine awareness.

Inequality Starts Young

In Iraq, as in many developing countries, a far smaller proportion of girls enrols in primary school compared to boys. In traditional value-systems or in areas of extreme poverty, it is often considered more important for a girl to stay at home and work. As a result, in many schools, girls are treated unfairly and made to feel unwelcome.

Throughout the world, UNICEF campaigns to make schools girl-friendly, including providing separate toilets, training more female teachers, and removing gender-bias from the textbooks used in schools.

FACTFILE: Education for All

Year: 1990

Occasion: World Conference on Education for All

Venue: Jomtien, Thailand

Present: UNICEF, UNESCO, UNDP, UNFPA, the World Bank and scores of agencies and NGOs (see acronym glossary page 46).

Goal: Education for All by the year 2000.

Result: By 2002, 82% of children, more than ever before, were enrolled in primary school. However, 120 million children still have no access to basic education, and 53% of these children are girls.

CHILD LABOUR

Firozabad in India is famous for its beautiful glass bangles, which are worn by every Indian girl and woman. The factories employ 200,000 people. Of these, 50,000 are children, working illegally, and earning less than 30 pence a day.

The bangle factories are dangerous places. The children risk being burned by the searing heat of the ovens, gashed by the spinning wheels which cut the glass, or catching a lung infection from the sharp particles of dust in the air. There is no first aid treatment available.

Throughout the developing world, 211 million children between the ages of 5 and 14 have to work, some for up to 16 hours a day. UNICEF and the ILO (the International Labour Organization) lead the worldwide campaign against child labour.

Terrible Treatment

Children work because their families are desperate for money, and they have no other options.

Worldwide, as many as 111 million children aged 5 to 14 work in hazardous conditions, in jobs involving toxic chemicals, dangerous machinery or heavy weights.

Some employers take children far from their homes and force them to live in terrible conditions. A study in the Philippines found working children being kept in cages.

Girls in Pakistan work at a loom. Long hours of carpet weaving can cause muscular diseases and deformities. ▼

"Dust from the chemical powders and strong vapours in both the store room and the boiler room were obvious .... We found 250 children, mostly below 10 years of age, working in a long hall filling in a slotted frame with sticks. Row upon row of children, some barely five years old, were involved in the work.**"**

From a report on the matchstick-making industry in Sivakasi, India

Other Forms of Child Labour

UNICEF is keen to point out that most working children are 'invisible'. Invisible workers include young girls in unpaid domestic work, or street-children scavenging amongst the rubbish. All these children are missing out on school.

Child labour is by no means restricted to the developing world. In the United Kingdom, for example, studies have shown that between 15 and 26 per cent of 11-year-olds and between 36 and 66 per cent of 15-year-olds work in full or part-time jobs.

The Need for an Alternative

It became clear during the early 1990s that merely forcing companies to stop employing children is not enough. When the US put immense pressure on Bangladesh to stop employing children in garment factories, thousands of child workers were dismissed. Many of them were girls.

Months later, most of them were working elsewhere, earning less money in more dangerous situations, including prostitution.

UNICEF's programmes aim to provide alternatives to child labour. These include encouraging employers to hire older members of a family, and establishing informal schools on work premises, so children can spend at least part of the day in education.

The single most effective way to stem the flow of school-age children into abusive forms of work is to improve and extend education, and to help poor families to send their children to school. In India, where it is estimated that 55 million children are working, the 'Joyful Learning Initiative' aims to make education more exciting and creative.

This boy in Brazil collects materials from rubbish dumps to sell to recyclers. ▼

Chapter Six:
UNICEF in the Community

UNICEF cannot work alone. In every one of its programmes, UNICEF co-operates with local and national governments, with private and state-owned companies, and with religious and cultural leaders. All of these have their own private aims. UNICEF must work together with them, and persuade them that the fight to save and protect all the world's children is the most important aim of all.

A POLITICAL TIGHTROPE

UNICEF is an Inter-Governmental Organization (IGO). It has to work together with national governments. Although it strives to be non-political in all of its work, in practice UNICEF sometimes finds it extremely difficult to avoid becoming involved in national and international politics.

Sometimes UNICEF can gently manipulate national politics to its own ends. During his tours of the developing world, James Grant persuaded many political leaders that children were a vote-winning issue.

Almost a quarter of UNICEF's funds are spent on advocacy – the continual struggle to persuade governments to change their laws

Many thousands of street children in Brazil are labouring, scavenging and even working as prostitutes to earn a living. ▼

In 1989 the Statute of the Child and Adolescent was approved by both houses of the National Congress, legally obligating the Brazilian Government to protect children's rights. Children were involved in gaining its acceptance, with more than 5,000 meeting in Brasilia. João de Deus, one of the organizers, recalls, **"**The day the children occupied the Senate was the most important day of my life...There were congressmen crying who gave up their seats to the children.**"**

and respect the rights of children. It must do this with great tact, so that those governments do not feel that their power is being called into question.

▲ A young boy sleeps on the street in Rio de Janeiro. Street children in Brazil are frequently treated as criminals by the police.

TIME FOR CHANGE IN BRAZIL

During the late 1980s, Brazil began to move towards democracy. When the new laws were drawn up in 1989, local NGOs, such as the National Street Children's Movement, campaigned to ensure a high priority for children. UNICEF gave them its full support.

A public campaign led to mass gatherings in cities. This pressure on the government led to the establishment of a National Committee on Children and the Constitution. UNICEF helped to get the Committee up and running.

Finally, the Brazilian Government established a statute. Children's rights became law. Councils for the Rights of the Child and Adolescent were set up at national, state and local levels. These Councils ensure that children's rights are upheld in all areas of Brazilian society. They are given money by the Government and they raise additional funds, all of which are used to help children and teenagers escape from life on the streets.

DERBY
DE22 1JD

◀ This Bangladeshi girl has goitre, an iodine deficiency disorder in which the thyroid gland swells. If her diet continues to lack iodine, her mental and physical growth will be severely affected.

One of UNICEF's most famous food-fortification campaigns is salt-iodization – adding iodine to salt. During the 1990s, the campaign was strongly supported by the Canadian Government. But to succeed, UNICEF had to persuade the salt producers, many of them old-fashioned state-owned enterprises, to put the lives of children above all other concerns.

FIGHTING MALNOURISHMENT

UNICEF aims to tackle, wherever possible, the root causes of a problem. In the case of malnutrition, UNICEF has scored some famous successes by working closely with commercial food suppliers to make dramatic changes to their businesses.

There are 200 million malnourished children in the world. Many of them are missing just one vital micronutrient in their diet, such as vitamin A, iron or iodine. In the 1970s, UNICEF and WHO realized that, if micronutrients could be added to basic foods at the manufacturing stage, large numbers of children's lives could be saved. This process is known as fortification.

Crippling Effects

Iodine, a micronutrient, is an essential ingredient of the diet of pregnant women and young children. Iodine helps the body to produce the hormones which are vital for a child to grow up healthily.

Iodine deficiency disorders (IDD) can lead to physical stunting and brain damage. In most cases, a lack of iodine in the diet of a pregnant woman will either kill her baby before it is born, or lead to lifelong mental disability for her child.

During the 1990s, UNICEF and the WHO's worldwide salt-iodization programmes have had astonishing results, but there are still 35 developing countries where less than half the population uses iodized salt.

Global Action

UNICEF's main task was to persuade salt producers to introduce an expensive new stage into their manufacturing processes. Salt producers were understandably worried that their salt would cost more than non-iodized salt, and people would stop buying it. Therefore, as part of their campaigns, UNICEF persuaded governments to make it illegal to import non-iodized salt. In addition, UNICEF campaigned for international trade agreements, to ensure that prices of iodized salt were competitive with non-iodized salt.

Goodwill Ambassadors

In 1994, the NGO Kiwanis International joined UNICEF's campaign to eliminate IDD. The Honorary Chairman of the joint UNICEF-Kiwanis Campaign is British actor Roger Moore, most famous for playing James Bond during the 1970s.

Roger Moore is one of several UNICEF Goodwill Ambassadors. These international celebrities give their time and money to campaign on behalf of UNICEF. Actors, musicians and sports stars such as Susan Sarandon, Robbie Williams and Manchester United's footballers have made a huge contribution to UNICEF.

FACTFILE: Salt-iodization

- The first salt was iodized in Switzerland in 1922.
- The campaign gathered momentum when in 1990 UNICEF identified the virtual elimination of IDD as an achievable goal. Now, almost 60% of the world's salt is iodized.
- In 1990, 120,000 children were born with cretinism - mental retardation caused by iodine deficiency. By 1997, that figure had been reduced by half to 60,000.
- UNICEF is still fighting to bring the figure down to zero.
- Iodized salt saves 12 million babies a year from retardation.
- Households in the developing world using iodized salt:
  - 1990: 20%
  - 2000: 70%

CIVIL WAR IN COLOMBIA

A brutal civil war has been tearing Colombia apart for forty years, threatening to traumatize a generation of children. The UNICEF-supported Children's Movement for Peace offers a ray of hope to Colombian children. It is one of the many pressure groups throughout the world which is supported by UNICEF.

Tragedy and Triumph

'When I was three years old, some men came to our house and murdered my parents and two-year-old brother.' Luisa Fernanda's experience left her alone in the world, and emotionally scarred for life. Sadly, her story is typical of the tens of thousands of children affected by Colombia's endless civil war.

Now, there is some hope for Luisa Fernanda and children like her. She, and around 100,000 Colombian children, have joined the Children's Movement for Peace. The Movement was set up by children in 1996, with the support of UNICEF, the Church, the Red Cross and other NGOs. Hundreds of children trained as counsellors, to help other children affected by violence. Membership soon swelled to include children from all across the country, regardless of their race or background. Children in Colombia have shown adults what can be achieved when people work together for a common purpose.

Colombian children wave flags reading 'peace' in Spanish. These festivities were organized by the Children's Movement for Peace. ▼

Luisa Fernanda, orphaned by the civil war in Colombia, talks about the Children's Movement for Peace:

"I think of it as an ever-expanding river, getting fuller and richer all the time. Our most important message is that children can be involved in peace building now, in our friendships and relationships, and by helping our communities. If you help other people then they will help you, and life will become better for everyone."

▲ Juan Elias Uribe, whose father was killed in the civil war, was one of the founding members of the Colombian Children's Movement for Peace.

No More Fighting?

One of the many achievements of the Children's Movement has been to set up thousands of 'Territories of Peace' throughout Colombia.

One such Territory of Peace is the community of Benposta, near the Colombian capital, Bogotá. Luisa Fernanda was welcomed there, after a lonely and frightening journey to Bogotá. In Benposta, she joined over 150 other children. Some are orphans, others have been abused, neglected and abandoned by their parents.

Benposta is an island of peace in a chaotic and violent country. The war in Colombia still goes on, but Luisa hopes that the Children's Movement will ensure a more peaceful future.

Protect the Children

Children have the right to participate in decisions about their lives. No child should be made to suffer in silence as a result of what adults do.

Throughout the world, tragedies such as child labour, war and AIDS force millions of children to suffer the pain of growing up alone.

By supporting causes such as the Colombian Children's Movement for Peace, UNICEF tries to help children to join together and share their experiences. Their work shows that, when children team up and work together, adults stop and listen, and there is a real possibility that change can take place.

Chapter Seven:
The Future

● ●

UNICEF is the only UN agency which is not restricted to a particular issue. To protect and save children, UNICEF has to undertake a much wider range of programmes than any other agency anywhere. Children's wellbeing is neither just a health issue, nor a food issue, nor an education issue, nor an anti-war issue, nor a human rights issue … it is all of these, and more.

DIVISION OF LABOUR

UNICEF's work overlaps considerably with other UN agencies, such as the WHO in the area of health, the International Labour Organization (ILO) in the area of child labour, and the World Food Program (WFP) in the area of nutrition. The division of responsibility between UNICEF and the WHO has been particularly blurred at times.

Despite this, co-operation between UNICEF and the WHO has proved extremely fruitful on a number of occasions. WHO provides high-level scientific research, advocacy and policy-planning. UNICEF, through its national committees and country

FACTFILE: Targets and Achievements

1990 TARGET
Goal 1: Reduce infant and under-5 mortality rate by 33%.

Goal 3: Between 1990 and the year 2000, reduction of severe and moderate malnutrition by half among children under 5.

Goal 4: Universal access to safe drinking water.

2000 ACHIEVEMENT
Goal 1: Achieved in 63 countries. Overall, an 11% reduction with three million fewer child deaths.

Goal 3: Over the decade, 18 countries including China, Indonesia and Bangladesh achieved remarkable reductions of 25% or more. However, many countries, particularly in South Asia and sub-Saharan Africa still have shockingly high levels of chronic malnutrition.

Goal 4: Goal not even neared. However, a 5% increase, with 900 million additional people having access to improved water supplies.

A UNICEF fieldworker in Angola teaches children about the dangers of landmines. Many countries have tens of thousands of landmines in the ground, and there are no maps to show where they are.

offices, can offer an unrivalled network throughout the world.

UNICEF has contact not only with NGOs, religious leaders, media organizations, companies and governments, but also with mothers, families, village health-workers, and most importantly, with children themselves. UNICEF can get to the heart of a problem in a way no other agency can.

NATIONS UNITED

At the 1990 World Summit for Children, UNICEF set itself and the world 27 specific targets in every area of its work, from sanitation to the outlawing of landmines.

By 1995, most of the mid-decade targets had been achieved, and some of the 2000 goals were well within reach. Some of the achievements were spectacular, especially in the areas of immunization, ORT usage and the fight against malnutrition. However, in the second half of the 1990s, progress slowed, and many of the goals were not achieved.

The goals were extremely ambitious, and as UNICEF tries to improve percentages, it is swimming against the tide of a massive population increase in the developing world. The HIV/AIDS pandemic has also played a part in setting back development. Additionally, changes in governments and health services that were not built to last meant that, after initial success, some of the good work was not sustained. UNICEF was reminded of the importance of putting lasting systems in place, to make change permanent.

Most of the goals have been extended to 2010 and beyond. The fight to realize them during the next few years continues as passionately as ever.

THE FUTURE

The 1990 World Summit for Children was a triumphant moment in the history of UNICEF. Countless world leaders promised to ratify the newly-drafted Convention on the Rights of the Child (CRC). Every country has ratified it except the US and Somalia. The US is still discussing how to reconcile the notion of children's rights with the traditional role of the family. Somalia does not have a coherent government.

Meena – UNICEF's animated cartoon heroine, who teaches children through films and on the internet about the rights of girls, particularly concerning education. ▼

All Children Are Equal

According to the Convention, every child in the world has the right to survive and develop free from unnecessary suffering, to be protected from abuse and to have control of their own lives. They also have responsibilities to respect the rights of others.

The Battle Goes On

The obstacles to UNICEF's work are larger than ever. Vicious wars still rage all over the world. AIDS is having a catastrophic effect on the lives of millions of children, and there is no sign that it is under control. Children's rights to education, freedom from exploitation and participation in decisions affecting their own lives are widely abused. The gap between rich and poor nations is increasing every year.

To succeed in the future, UNICEF needs to maintain the vision, passion and sheer effort which has characterized its work since 1946, and which led former UN Secretary General Perez de Cuellar to describe UNICEF as 'the jewel in the crown' of the UN.

UNICEF must persuade rich countries to dedicate a fraction more of their vast budgets to overseas aid. It must find ever more inventive ways to promote its

▲ Children are seen and heard at the UN Special Session for Children in 2002.

• •

work and raise funds. Most importantly, it must keep its roots firmly in the field, so it can help suffering children wherever they are.

The Grand Alliance

In May 2002, the UN held a Special Session on Children, during which world leaders again committed themselves and their countries to a set of goals. Children from more than 100 nations took part and delivered a 700-word message to world leaders. This was the first time children had ever directly addressed the UN General Assembly.

Part of the message from children to world leaders, delivered at the 2002 UN Special Session On Children:

❝ We are not the sources of problems; we are the resources that are needed to solve them. We are not expenses; we are investments. We promise that as adults we will defend children's rights with the same passion that we have now as children. We are the children of the world, and despite our different backgrounds, we share a common reality. We are united by our struggle to make the world a better place for all. You call us the future, but we are also the present. ❞

More people in the world than ever before are aware of UNICEF's work. More children than ever before are involved in the fight for their rights.

ORGANIZATIONS AND ACRONYMS

IGO Inter-Governmental Organization (organizations made up of at least three nations, based on a formal agreement between them, e.g.: the European Union).

ILO International Labour Organization.

NGO Non-Governmental Organization (organizations that work independently from governments, e.g.: OXFAM).

UN United Nations

UNDP United Nations Development Programme

UNESCO United Nations Educational, Scientific, and Cultural Organization

UNFPA United Nations Population Fund

UNICEF United Nations Children's Fund

WHO World Health Organization

WORLD BANK An international organization that helps the economic development of developing countries

WORDS

advocacy Supporting or campaigning in favour of a cause, idea or policy.

AIDS Acquired Immune Deficiency Syndrome: a disease that seriously weakens the immune system.

anaemia A disease in which the sufferer does not have enough red blood cells.

antenatal clinic A clinic giving health checks to pregnant women.

cholera A disease of the digestive system, carried by bacteria in dirty water or food.

Convention A general agreement between nations: less formal than a treaty.

delegate A representative sent by a group or nation to a conference.

democracy A system of government in which leaders are elected by the people.

developing countries Countries with low living standards and poor basic services.

development The process by which poorer countries experience a growth in average income and move to an economy based on industry.

diarrhoea A common symptom of digestive diseases. The body tries to flush out infections by passing large volumes of water, leading to dehydration.

discrimination Unfair treatment based on race, religion, age or sex.

donor fatigue The feeling that donations to IGOs and NGOs are not making any difference.

dysentery A disease of the intestine, common in areas of poor sanitation, which leads to very severe diarrhoea.

food-fortification The process of adding nutrients to food.

HIV Human Immunodeficiency Virus – the virus which leads to AIDS in humans.

IDD Iodine Deficiency Disorders – the illnesses that result from insufficient levels of the mineral iodine in the diets of embryos, babies and children.

illiterate Unable to read and write.

immunization Protecting against a disease, often by means of injections.

industrialized countries Countries with economies based on industry.

landmine A small explosive device buried just below the surface of the ground. Landmines explode if they are disturbed by contact, or even by vibration.

legislation A law or group of laws.

malnutrition Ill health resulting from an inadequate diet.

neonatal A word used to descibe a baby up to the first four weeks of its life.

nutrient An essential dietary substance.

pandemic A word used to describe a disease which affects people across a wide geographical area.

pressure group A group of people who try actively to influence legislation.

prostitute Someone who offers sex in return for money.

ratification The process by which a government agrees to change its national laws in accordance with a convention.

refugee Someone forced to run away from their home as a result of war, persecution, natural disaster or famine.

rehydration Replacing water and fluids lost by the body.

resource Anything that fulfils a need.

retardation Incomplete human growth.

rickets A children's disease caused by vitamin D deficiency. The bones become soft and do not grow properly.

sanitation Hygienic disposal of sewage.

smallpox A very infectious viral disease.

statute An act of law.

stillbirth The birth of a dead foetus.

summit Meeting of heads of government.

sustainable development Development which does not use up resources without replacing them.

tuberculosis An infectious disease which attacks the lungs.

Under-5 mortality rate In a given area, the number of children under the age of 5 out of every thousand who die.

vaccine A substance which gives the body protection against diseases.

yaws A children's skin disease.

FURTHER READING

BOOKS FOR YOUNGER READERS
Children Just Like Me Dorling Kindersley/UNICEF, 1995

BOOKS FOR OLDER READERS
Out of War: True Stories from the Frontline of the Children's Movement for Peace in Colombia Sara Cameron/ Scholastic, 2001
For Every Child Caroline Castle (adapted, with a foreword by Archbishop Desmond Tutu), Phyllis Fogelman Books, 2000
A Life Like Mine Dorling Kindersley/ UNICEF, 2002
Facts for Life UNICEF and other agencies, 2002, provides information on the main causes of childhood illness and death. It can be downloaded from: http://www.unicef.org/ffl/

USEFUL ADDRESSES
UNICEF
UNICEF House, 3 United Nations Plaza
New York, NY 10017

The United Kingdom Committee for UNICEF
Africa House, 64-78 Kingsway
London WC2B 6NB
Tel 0870 606 3377